THE TWO DIALOGUES:

Interior and Interpersonal
Questions That Build
Hope and Community

DONALD EGGLESTON, M.ED, M.DIV

The Two Dialogues:
Questions That Build Hope and Community
Don Eggleston, M Ed, M Div
Mission Works Publishing, LLC

Design: Lopez Needleman Graphic Design, Inc., St. Louis, Missouri, 314.647.6308, jean@lopezneedleman.com, www.lopezneedleman.com

Library of Congress Cataloging-in-Publication Data
Don Eggleston
The Two Dialogues: Questions That Build Hope and Community
ISBN: 978-0-9997417-1-9 (paperback)
Library of Congress subject headings:
  1. BUS085000 Business & Economics / Organizational Behavior
  2. OCC019000 Body, Mind & Spirit / Inspiration & Personal Growth
  3. SEL021000 Self-Help / Motivational & Inspirational

2021

September 2021, Mission Works Publishing.

WITH GRATITUDE TO:

John O'Leary: The embodiment of courage
Dr. Tom Wagner: Fostering resilience
Dr. John Wickersham: Teacher and storyteller
Dr. Harry Bradley: Model of the two dialogues
Kathy Buchheit, FSM: Birth and re-birth
Jean Lopez: Art and soul
Mary Ann Eggleston: Ever optimistic, fun and lifegiving

WORDS
CREATE
WORLDS.

– Rabbi Abraham Joshua Heschel

HOW TO USE THIS BOOK

The Two Dialogues is intended to provide an opportunity for self-reflection and to serve as *guidebook*. In these pages, you will have the opportunity to develop enhanced self-knowledge and transformative relationships with others through:

- Ideas from my personal experience and the distilled approaches of other authors;
- Scripture passages for prayerful reflection;
- Questions which I have developed and used which can be adapted by you to build your relationships with family, friends, students, teachers, professional colleagues, and even strangers.

INTRODUCTION

Abraham Joshua Heschel (1907-1972) was a Polish-born American rabbi, philosopher and theologian. As a young man, he escaped from Nazi-held Europe, but his mother and two of his sisters were murdered during the Holocaust. He eventually became an advocate and activist in the American civil rights movement. When asked how he transformed the pain of losing his immediate family at the hands of despots into his involvement on behalf of those without access to adequate housing, voting rights, and educational systems, he uttered three words: "Words create worlds." He explained that during his lifetime the words spoken about both Jews and African Americans created worlds where exclusion, defamation, and extermination became a reality. Conversely, when we engage each other around words that elevate and affirm one another, the transformation of the human condition is possible.

The word "dialogue" comes from the Greek language and translates: "To speak through, to speak meaning." The object of dialogue is NOT to win an argument or to exchange opinions. The object is to listen to one another and to achieve mutual understanding and beneficial change. This is rapidly becoming an outdated concept in a social media-driven culture where one's "posts" can replace truly listening to another.

For decades now, people have called for an increase in dialogue in politics and academic circles, as well as between races and generations. How do we achieve dialogue and a flow of meaning in cultural crossroads like politics, religion, workplaces, classrooms, health centers, and in any setting where race, gender, viewpoints, and lifestyle intersect?

How do our words create worlds with and among us?

Have you ever had a conversation with a friend, family member, work colleague, student, teacher or even a stranger – that you remember to this day? I have and, in fact, it has happened numerous times in the above settings.

TWO EXAMPLES:

Two years ago, I asked at the conclusion of a university class I was teaching: "What are you thinking about *now* that you were not thinking about before today's class?" (I often ask this question to help students to apply class material and to informally evaluate the effectiveness of instruction.) Frequently, the responses are focused on the topic we discussed or on an exercise we did. On this evening, one of the students remarked: "Some things that one of the other students said over the past few sessions made me realize that I am judging her without knowing her." I had the good sense to not respond and rather wait to see what happened. Shortly thereafter, two other students said the same thing. The four of them met the following weekend for coffee. Words create worlds...

While facilitating a retreat for a group of religious brothers and lay ministers I took a walk with one of the brothers who asked for a little time. At first, we talked about the retreat, his childhood, etc. until he finally said what was on his heart: "I want to use this time to share something that I am carrying, that feels like a weight inside." He proceeded to tell me about the years he spent in Africa as a teacher and missionary. He spoke of the civil war and atrocities he had witnessed. He admitted he had not taken advantage of the "re-entry"

How do our words create worlds with and among us?

7

resources he was offered and how the memory of what he experienced was impacting his daily life. We were able to connect him with professionals who could help. When he found the courage to speak the words, he found the path to the healing he needed and deserved. Words create worlds...

Each of these experiences were distinguished by an act of *vulnerability* which is the very heart of *dialogue* with others. Henri Nouwen, in his book *Reaching Out*, stated that "What is most personal is most universal and indeed nothing human is strange to us." He speaks in most of his books about how our vulnerability reveals our innermost thoughts and feelings — our worries, uncertainties, doubts, regrets, discoveries — and how the sharing of vulnerability actually builds community.

> "What is most personal is most universal and indeed nothing human is strange to us." – Henri Nouwen

THE MAN WITH A WITHERED HAND (MATTHEW 12:9-14)

Like any account of the ministry of Jesus, this passage is ripe with opportunities for learning and application. The evident struggle in this situation is between Jesus and the religious leaders who questioned his authority. He was challenged around whether he should perform a healing miracle on the sabbath. What is important to know about this story is the commonly-held belief about *illness* in the day. Illness was seen as a punishment, a sign of disfavor, the result of sin. And so, at first glance, when Jesus tells the young man in the story to reach out his hand, it looks like an act of humiliation and thoughtlessness. This is actually the *turning point* of the story, the declaration that all is not well in this man's life. It is this act of vulnerability, the *literal* and *figurative* stretching out of his hand, that allows a deep, deep healing to occur.

James Keenan is a Jesuit priest, bioethicist, moral theologian, and writer. In his writing, he defines the act of showing *mercy* as "the willingness to enter into the *chaos* of another person." This interpretation of mercy removes the definition from a "better than to lower than" equation. Mercy is no longer extended only from the rich to the poor, the better educated to the poorly educated, the better housed to the poorly housed... Entering into the chaos of another is not a socioeconomic phenomenon only. We are *all* in chaos at various points in our lives. Entering the chaos of another is rooted in vulnerability, in declaring that all is not well. True transformational *dialogue* with another human being builds its foundation and sinks its roots in the fertile soil of *vulnerability*.

> True transformational dialogue with another human being builds its foundation and sinks its roots in the fertile soil of vulnerability.

THE
FIRST
DIALOGUE

Interior Questions that
Build Self-Awareness

What is a common disciplinary practice with a misbehaving child? Send them to their room, correct? What if we chose to send kids to their room as a *reward* for *positive* behavior?

Having a *quiet center*, a quiet interior core, is something to be sought after. Solitude is *not* loneliness. Solitude is part of one's life stance whereby we experience the world around us with gratitude, attention, and compassion.

> "Life without a quiet center easily becomes delusional."

The person who wrote this line was Henri Nouwen. Nouwen was a renowned Dutch priest and author, respected professor, and beloved pastor. Henri taught at the University of Notre Dame and at the Divinity Schools of Yale and Harvard. He lived and worked with Trappist monks. He states in several of his books that he dealt with periodic burnout and depression. He went on to write that it was in living and working in a community for developmentally disabled adults called L'Arche ("The Ark") that he experienced the gift of solitude *and* community. Living in a Trappist monastery lit the flame of solitude but it was in a home for developmentally disabled adults that solitude

and community came together. "Life without a quiet center easily becomes delusional."

With the help of modern technology, we can reach people all over the world with the touch of our fingers. During the COVID-19 pandemic we have seen our electronic devices become the means to work together, to educate, to celebrate milestones, and to share our burdens. We have also witnessed these devices being used to spew hatred, mistruth, and almost constant outrage. "Life without a quiet center easily becomes delusional." If we are not mindful, we will function almost exclusively in the *external* realm, chasing posts and blogs, and seeking "likes" without the benefit of a reflective, calm, necessary separateness that an interior life affords us.

ONE RESOURCE: "YOUR INNER ROOMMATE"

Michael Singer is an author and meditation practitioner who wrote a book titled The *Untethered Soul; The Journey Beyond Yourself.* In one of the key sections, Singer discusses the importance of "dialing down" (my term) the "inner roommate," that voice inside of us that bogs us down with unrelenting self-criticism and self-doubt. Utilizing his "roommate" image, Singer asks his readers what they would do if they actually had a roommate who constantly questioned their appearance, their intellectual capacities, their capacity to achieve goals, and so on. If the roommate persisted with behavior of this sort, he reasons, it would be best for one of us to "move out."

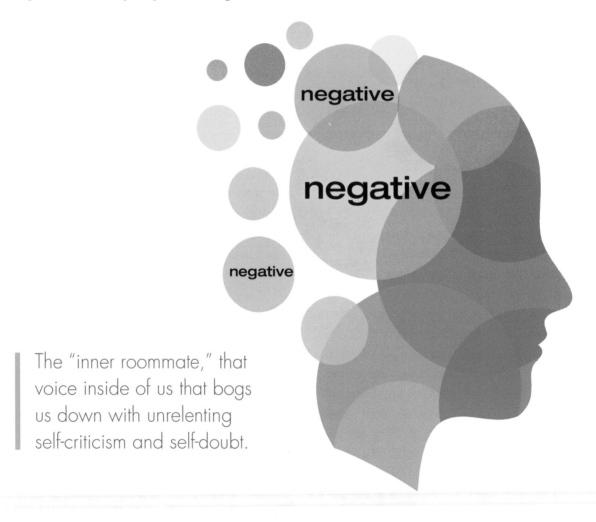

The "inner roommate," that voice inside of us that bogs us down with unrelenting self-criticism and self-doubt.

QUESTIONS TO CONSIDER:

1. What messages or thoughts do I carry within me that are damaging to my image of myself?

    _____

    _____

    _____

    _____

2. How do my negative thoughts affect my confidence in my personal and professional relationships?

    _____

    _____

    _____

    _____

3. How do my negative thoughts distract me from listening to others and being supportive of them?

    _____

    _____

    _____

    _____

4. What are some consequences of being excessively critical of myself?

    _____

    _____

    _____

    _____

| "Signature strengths" represent the core virtues at work in our lives.

ANOTHER RESOURCE: "YOUR SIGNATURE CHARACTER STRENGTHS"

Martin Seligman, a psychologist from the University of Pennsylvania, is the author of several books, including *Learned Helplessness* and *Authentic Happiness*. Along with his research colleagues, Seligman spent years reading and synthesizing scientific and religious discussions of *good character*. Together, they developed what they call "signature strengths" that represent the core virtues at work in our lives. Together they developed the VIA Survey of Character Strengths. The survey is free of charge and over 13 million people have completed it world-wide. It is a psychometrically validated personality test that measures an individual's character strengths. The premise of the survey is when you discover your greatest strengths, you can use them to face life's challenges, work toward goals, and feel more fulfilled personally and professionally. You can access the survey at "VIA Character Strengths Survey." You may consider stopping and taking it before reading the rest of this section; it takes about 20 minutes to complete. Along with the summary of your signature strengths, you will be offered strategies for developing those strengths more fully.

For purposes of example, my top five signature strengths are:

1. Gratitude ("Awareness of the good things happening in my life and never taking these for granted.")
2. Capacity to love and be loved (Valuing close relationships with others.")
3. Love of learning ("Love learning new things whether in a classroom, book, or interaction.")
4. Kindness and generosity ("Generous toward others, never too busy to do a favor, even to strangers.")
5. Spirituality, sense of purpose and faith. ("Strong and coherent beliefs about the higher purpose and meaning of life.")

Can you see what a gift it is to complete a survey that focuses on your strengths and capacities? Many organizations, including the United States military, make use of this survey. I have used the VIA survey in classroom and team-based settings, accompanying it with exploratory questions that give it substance and ready application.

QUESTIONS TO CONSIDER:

1. Is there a situation where I can bring one of my strengths to bear in a helpful way?

_____

_____

_____

_____

2. Do any of my strengths ever function as a limitation? (For example, my strength of kindness and generosity can lead me to being taken advantage of and can lead to resentment when I overcommit.)

_____

_____

_____

_____

3. Is anyone or anything preventing me from using one of my strengths? Are the behaviors of others or the messages from my "inner roommate" impeding me in any way?

_____

_____

_____

_____

"EXTRA CREDIT"

One question for additional reflection: What is a quality that I possess (i.e. kindness, humor, determination, creativity) that is so easily seen in me that if I lost this quality, I would be unrecognizable to those who know me?

_____

THE STILL, SMALL VOICE OF GOD (I KINGS 10:1-18)

Elijah had just successfully completed a dramatic confrontation with the worshippers of the god Baal. However, he quickly went from being a hero to being the object of Queen Jezebel's desire to kill him for being what she viewed as a troublesome prophet.

Fearing for his life, Elijah's travels ultimately return him to Mount Horeb. The name Horeb evokes images of God as powerful and awe-provoking, overthrowing kingdoms and restoring the downtrodden. Elijah rightfully expects God's consolation in an overpowering way — in the wind, in an earthquake, in fire. Ironically, Elijah was drawn out of his hiding place by "the still, small voice of God," in the subtle, undramatic, consoling stillness.

It is this same stillness that came to St. Francis of Assisi and St. Ignatius of Loyola in their recovery from battlefield injuries and capture that led to solitude, reflection, and conversion to a new path. It is the same stillness that Thomas Merton found in a monastery and that Mother Teresa found in quiet prayer. Solitude prepared them for their journeys of forming community in service of others.

As a practical step in helping clients in his counseling practice, a clinical psychologist friend of mine routinely asks his clients to limit their use of social media and 24-hour news channels in order to reduce anxiety and distraction. Give this a try: disregard the "earthquakes" and "storms" and listen for the still voice within you, the voice of self-acceptance leading to remarkable gratitude and generosity.

> Elijah was drawn out of his hiding place by "the still, small voice of God," in the subtle, undramatic, consoling stillness.

THE
SECOND
DIALOGUE

Interpersonal Questions
that Build Community

Building on the "First Dialogue," a foundation of self-reflection, self-awareness, and a rich interior life, we are then ready to enter into a rich dialogue with others. When effectively done, dialogue with others is characterized by vulnerability, exploration, listening, and human progress. Transformational change in organizations can begin with a simple, single conversation. In your own life, a decision to commit to a spouse or partner, the selection of a workplace team, a substance abuse intervention, a mentoring relationship, are built upon authentic dialogue, on the decision to speak to meaning. As stated earlier, effective internal and interpersonal dialogue leads to thoughtful, beneficial action.

In this second half of the book, I am trying to achieve what educator, activist, and author, Parker Palmer called "a bridge between our soul and our role."

This section of the book will focus on the building of conversational structures that build understanding, collaboration, and commitment. Effective interpersonal dialogue can be awkward but with an intentional purpose and structure, incredible breakthroughs are possible.

I will provide questions that foster effective dialogue in the following settings:
- the workplace;
- within community and social movements;
- personal relationships;
- among different generations, races, orientations, and backgrounds;
- education.

The primary stance to take in these settings is to listen, to resist the urge to defend your position, and to become intent on establishing enduring relationships, solutions, and hope.

> When effectively done, dialogue with others is characterized by vulnerability, exploration, listening, and human progress.

COME TO THE OTHER SIDE OF THE BOAT — JOHN 21:1-9

I acknowledge that both sets of dialogue questions ask a lot of us. That's because *true dialogue* asks a lot of us.

From my days of seminary study, there were some beneficial outcomes: Development of an increased desire to serve people, enduring friendships, several inspiring teachers, and an appreciation for the complexity, consolation, and discomforting challenges of Judeo-Christian Scriptures.

One of my favorite Scripture passages (and one that I hope serves our purpose in enhancing dialogue *within ourselves* and *with others*) comes from the Gospel of John, where Jesus invites his disciples to "come to the other side of the boat."

The setting is the Sea of Tiberias, a name given to the Sea of Galilee by the Roman occupiers of Israel. After a night (the time of symbolic and real uncertainty for fishermen) that yielded nothing, the disciples meet Jesus in the *beginning of the day*, the beginning of literal and symbolic enlightenment. The disciples are told by Jesus to cast their nets to the other side of the boat to shed the efforts and activity that only produced cynicism and disbelief.

We're often asked in life to *come to the other side of the boat*. We see this in people who daily seek and sustain sobriety, in people who shed unwanted self-doubt and self-criticism, in people who resist stereotypes, and, certainly in being willing to *listen, listen, listen* to another human being.

> We're often asked in life to come to the other side of the boat

ASK THESE "TEST-DRIVEN" QUESTIONS when facilitating conversations in workplaces, classrooms, neighborhood associations, churches and other organizations in transition — and with people of different races, genders, ages, and backgrounds. I have found these questions to be valuable in helping to build trust and promote listening, especially in situations where conflict is present, or just under the surface.

- What is something that you wish others would not presume about you because of your age, race, educational level, appearance, or occupation?
- What was a difficult period in your life and how did you deal with it? What qualities did you develop as a result of this challenging time?
- What is a gift or talent you have within you that others overlook when they judge you superficially?

I have found that when you ask questions of this magnitude, it is important to *just listen*. Often, the next question comes to you out of this listening. Margaret Wheatley is an American writer who holds a doctorate in Education with a focus on Administration, Policy and Social Policy from the Harvard Graduate School of Education. As a young woman she also served in the Peace Corps. She proposes that "real social change comes from the ageless process of people thinking together in conversation." A quotation from her at the end of her book, *Turning to One Another: Simple Conversations to Restore Hope to the Future*, she writes: "You don't fear people whose story you know."

While we have all had memorable, striking conversations with others that emerge spontaneously and have lasting impact, in situations where the stakes are high and conflict is anticipated, asking an intentional, deliberate set of questions is truly beneficial. When you ask questions that are structured, the *authenticity* of the questions wins out, whether in a workplace, a classroom, a crucial political community setting, or in personal relationships.

I enjoyed a 30-year career in healthcare and worked in community health outreach, organizational development, and mission integration in an organization of 30,000 employees. Mission Integration is a leadership function that is essentially "owned" by every member of an organization. In faith-based healthcare, where I worked, the mission is reflected in:

- How patients and their loved ones are treated regardless of background, lifestyle-attributed illness, or their ability to pay.
- How ethical decisions are made at both clinical and operational levels.
- How the organization's values are found in the diagnosis, clinical treatment, and spiritual care of patients.
- How employees are able to find meaning in their work and how emotional and spiritual care is extended to them.
- How the leadership team is formed in the mission and charism of the founders of the organization and in the faith tradition that resides at the core of the organization.

Staying true to organization mission cannot be left to happenstance. It requires intention, diligence, measurement, nurturing of staff, and developing managers into leaders of ongoing organizational transformation. The following are questions that I asked in department meetings, individual conversations, due diligence meetings, and in moments of both political and real conflict. The application of these questions is not limited to healthcare.

1. **As a leader, what do I do day-to-day that makes your work easier or more *difficult*?** (This question yielded great information and kept me focused and humble. For example, I was told that one thing I did that made work *easier* was my willingness to share credit for all departmental achievements. What made work more *difficult* was me typing on my laptop while supposedly listening to others.)

2. **In the past week/month, what has occurred in our department/organization that convinces you that the *mission and values* are alive and well?** (If your employees do not know the organization's mission and values, you have another challenge.)

3. **Tell me something about your organization's culture that, if it were to disappear in our new structure, it would be a doggone shame?** In facilitating an acquisition or merger (in addition to all the operational due diligence questions), I found this question yielded a remarkable amount of *information* and *optimism*.

4. **What led you to join this organization? What keeps you here on your most difficult day?**

5. **What qualities do you possess that we are not utilizing in our organization?**

6. (When correcting or encouraging) **What do you think is the impact of your behavior?** (i.e., mentoring a colleague vs. being sarcastic toward a co-worker; showing willingness to join a work team vs. regularly being late for or disruptive in meetings)

7. **In addressing performance issues,** I derived great benefit from the following conversation points I developed over my years in leadership:

- **Here's what _I've_ done to make you successful** (i.e., provided coaching and orientation, giving you a developmental assignment, introduced you to key people, etc.)
- **What have you done to make yourself successful?**
- **Here's what I expect you to do without fail.**
- **What additional support do you want from me?**
- **If these results do not occur, the following consequences will take place.**

Staying true to organization mission… requires intention, diligence, measurement, nurturing of staff, and developing managers into leaders of ongoing organizational transformation.

MARTHA AND MARY — LUKE 10:31-42

This passage at first reading looks like a clear-cut message: Be like Mary, one who sits at the feet of her guest, Jesus, and learns from him. Don't be like Martha, doing so many tasks to get ready for Jesus, that she misses out on the significance of his teachings. In fact, Mary and Martha each want the *same thing*. They each want Jesus to *act* upon them, to *see* them and to touch their hearts.

Right *before* this passage in Luke, the disciples ask Jesus: "Teach us to pray." What follows is what we now call "The Lord's Prayer." They are essentially asking Jesus to reveal the wonder of his *discoveries*, his *depth*, his *compelling presence*. And so, they ask: "Teach us to pray."

Right after this story of Martha and Mary comes the parable of the Good Samaritan, the ultimate statement of discipleship as *service*. The Trappist monk, Thomas Merton, reinforces the need for a harmony between action and reflection in his book *Contemplation in a World of Action* when he writes: "He who attempts to do things for others or for the world without deepening his own self-understanding, freedom, integrity, and capacity to love — will not have anything to give to others."

"He who attempts to do things for others or for the world without deepening his own self-understanding, freedom, integrity, and capacity to love — will not have anything to give to others." – Thomas Merton

QUESTIONS FOR TEACHERS/FACILITATORS

I have served as a teacher/facilitator in many settings over the course of my career: high school (Be ready for questions!), university, post-graduate seminars, executive development, seminars and retreats. The questions that follow have helped to structure an environment of *discovery, encouragement*, and *joy*.

- Who was the best teacher you ever had and how did she/he help you learn?
- What is something you found to be *discouraging* in your educational experience?
- What do we expect of each other as teacher *and* student? What behaviors will we exhibit toward each other that will foster true learning?
- (At the end of a seminar/class) What is something you are aware of or wondering about now that you were not aware of before we gathered today/this week?
- Is there something another participant said or did that affected you favorably?
- As a teacher, what can I do to help you understand our subject?
- As a student, what can you do to be successful?
- (For faculty, staff, and administration) Where do we see our values and mission in our daily work?

Structure an environment of discovery, encouragement, and joy.

QUESTIONS FOR ELECTED OFFICIALS WHO WANT TO BE ROLE MODELS

I propose here that elected officials at any level become role models for the populace by stepping away from the focus on their "base" and their Political Action Committee donors to become role models of constructive, fruitful dialogue. In engaging with the elected representative of a different party, or another committee member, the following questions can be helpful:

- What leads you to hold this belief? (Which personal experience? What validated research? What source(s)?)
- What are the strengths of your viewpoint and what are the possible limitations?
- What are the strengths of my viewpoints and what are the possible limitations?
- What is a proposal that would reflect the best of both of our ideas on this matter?

These four questions, possibly done over a cup of coffee without a team of staffers, foster civil dialogue that can lead to results larger and more beneficial than either person or group first thought possible. Come to the other side of the boat.

Become role models of constructive, fruitful dialogue

LET US PICK UP
THE STONES
OVER WHICH
WE STUMBLE,
FRIENDS, AND
BUILD ALTARS.

– Pádraig Ó Tuama

APPLYING THE TWO DIALOGUES:
A PERSONAL AND PROFESSIONAL EXAMPLE

A Personal Example

Without a doubt, my favorite sport is baseball. I love the strategy, the requisite physical and mental skill sets, and the science involved in a pitcher gripping and releasing a baseball in ways that deceive a batter.

I also appreciate the artistry involved when a batter connects with a pitch on the sweet spot on the bat. The sweet spot is the precise place on the bat that results in maximum energy being applied when the ball is struck. When a batter connects with a pitch on the sweet spot the ball travels at its fastest and, often, its furthest.

When I am living in an emotional and spiritual sweet spot, I enjoy insights into life, am aware of my personal gifts, make good decisions, avoid overcommitting myself and enjoy a deep sense of gratitude for blessings big and small.

For even the best hitters in the game of baseball, the sweet spot is elusive and a batter has to revisit his mental and physical approach to hitting in order to sustain success.

When I am not in an emotional or spiritual "zone," when the sweet spot is elusive, I have a tendency to worry about things that I cannot control and to be self-critical. My "inner roommate" worries about such things as a small variation on a medical test result or dwells too long on a single criticism on a class evaluation. When uneasy feelings of this sort arise I try to pause, take some deep breaths and try to identify where my anxiety is coming from and if my feelings are warranted at the "volume" level I am giving to them. This is a First Dialogue undertaking.

On the "Second Dialogue" level, when a particular source of anxiety is of an intensity or duration that I have trouble managing, I share my feelings with a friend or a trusted colleague and await their insights and perspectives. During certain periods in my life, I have sought the expertise of a therapist, a grief support group or another trained resource person.

In these personal instances, my first step is to go inward through solitude, prayer and relaxation exercises in pursuit of a guiding spirit, a Holy Spirit of insight and reassurance. Oftentimes, this process does wonders; at other times, the help of a wider community of support is needed.

The interior and interpersonal dialogues also can be a way to grow a greater spirit of gratitude. On a daily basis, I intentionally make myself aware of the reasons for gratitude in my life: a beautiful scene in nature, a call from a friend, a roof over my head, or a meal in front of me. On the heels of this interior exercise, when another person is the source of my gratitude, I make it a point to tell that person with a phone call, email or a good old-fashioned handwritten note. Thus, this internally-felt blessing forms an interpersonal bond. In doing this gratitude exercise, I become grateful for smaller and smaller things and many of my anxieties lessen.

> The interior and interpersonal dialogues can be a way to grow a greater spirit of gratitude.

A Professional Example

At different points in my career, I worked as an organizational development consultant. In this role, I assisted groups with the development of strategies and goals, designing quality improvement initiatives , and building policies and practices which credibly represented an organization's mission and values. I also was asked on many occasions to work with groups where conflicts had diminished the effectiveness of a group or department.

In one instance, I worked with the staff of a hospital intensive care unit. These units require a tremendous number of employees. Patients require close scrutiny because their well-being can change abruptly. Effective communication with family members is crucial. There is a continuous learning curve due to new technology, the exposure to many procedures and medical interventions, and the influx of specialists and multi-disciplinary teams.

In this particular instance, communication between two shifts in the ICU became ineffective and, thus, conflict increased within the group.

Initially, I interviewed members of the department and determined multiple reasons for the conflict, among them work processes that never seemed to be "fixed," inadequate orientation to technology, and the failure to discuss frustrations that occurred within the group when a shift change occurred.

When it came to addressing the interpersonal judgments and assumptions that occurred between the two groups, I did not want to get bogged down in finger-pointing or any other intervention that only confirms suspicions and drives down trust.

Instead, I chose to ask two questions in small groups. These questions were:

1. **In this work setting or in a place where you worked previously, what was it like when the group was functioning at it's best? What did it look like when things were at their best in:**
   - **Communication between shifts**
   - **Raising concerns or issues that need to be addressed**
   - **Orientation of new co-workers**
   - **Getting help from each other at peak times**
   - **Supporting each other at difficult times**
   - **Building on the gifts and experience of each person**

Asking these questions in this way helped to bypass conversations that only intensify dislike for others and foster ongoing resentment.

2. **IF we were at our best as a team, what would it look like when it comes to:**
   - **Encouraging each other**
   - **Addressing an issue before the situation worsens**
   - **Appreciating the background and experiences of each co-worker**

Questions of this type enable people to shift from the interior dialogue (i.e., "They think they're better than us," or "They never recognize how our shift is more complicated than theirs," etc.) to an interpersonal one focused on building processes that create optimal functioning within a team. From this deliberative process, we were able to establish interpersonal behaviors that everyone agreed to follow, such as:

- "We will thank each other for assistance given."
- "We will touch base with each other whenever we leave the unit, offering an estimated time away from the center and identifying any questions that might arise while we are gone."
- "When an issue arises with a co-worker, we will identify within ourselves what we see as the impact of the person's behavior, go directly to the person in a private location and refuse to discuss anything behind the person's back."

- "We will make ourselves available to new co-workers and point out to them where they are making great progress."
- "We will celebrate milestones (graduations, recovery of patients, etc) with each other."

While these may seem like pretty basic guidelines, in groups that underperform interpersonally, these behaviors are typically absent. By enabling the group to do some interior work, the interpersonal relationships improved noticeably. Three and six month follow meetings confirmed the improvements.

This is a very different strategy from a head-on "tell us how much you dislike those people" approach. To the contrary, determining the strengths of the group (What does it look like when we are at our best?") and identifying what it would take to reduce divisiveness (if we were at our best?") significant improvement in interpersonal functioning were achieved.

In short, it takes conscious effort of this sort to change unconscious behavior.

It takes conscious effort to change unconscious behavior.

CONCLUSION

We have the capacity to *build* and *heal* each other *or* to diminish and demoralize each other.

True, humble curious dialogue creates memorable, authentic, and enduring experiences. As those experiences are built upon, credible, actionable avenues for change within the human heart and the greater human community emerge. Encounter builds upon encounter.

Now that you have seen how words can create worlds, choose to use your words to create the world we all deserve. Not everyone will be ready for this kind of dialogue. And yet, try. Have the courage to use these questions to make change in one setting, in one relationship, with one person. Start a conversation and listen at a different level than you did before. Take action to have real conversation be a part of your everyday life. Words create worlds...

TRUST THAT
MEANINGFUL
CONVERSATION
CAN CHANGE
YOUR WORLD.

– Margaret Wheatley

ABOUT THE AUTHOR

 Donald Eggleston is the founder of Mission Works, LLC, a teaching and consulting resource in support of the achievement of organizational mission and purpose. He also is the author of *With All We Are: Mission, purpose and transformation.*

Don enjoyed a 30-year career in health care; serving in the areas of community outreach and organizational development, and concluded his career as vice president of Mission Integration for SSM Health in St. Louis, MO.

He holds a Master of Divinity degree from Kenrick Seminary, a Master's Degree in Education from the University of Missouri — St. Louis, and has completed a certificate in Leadership of Organizational and Social Change from Case Western University.

Don welcomes your thoughts and questions at doneggleston6@gmail.com

CPSIA information can be obtained
at www.ICGtesting.com
Printed in the USA
BVHW052046241021
619747BV00003B/91